Made with Love

SWEETJULIAN.CO

The Lord

is on my side

I will not

Fear

PSALM 118:6

Tiny Blessing

Mighty Little One

DATE:

BABY'S WEIGHT TODAY: DAYS IN NICU:

CARES + HOLDING:

PROCEDURES:

NOTES + THOUGHTS:

Mighty Little One

TODAY I AM GRATEFUL FOR:

PRAYERS FOR PREEMIE:

Mighty Little One

DATE:

BABY'S WEIGHT TODAY: DAYS IN NICU:

CARES + HOLDING:

PROCEDURES:

NOTES + THOUGHTS:

Mighty Little One

TODAY I AM GRATEFUL FOR:

PRAYERS FOR PREEMIE:

Mighty Little One

DATE:

BABY'S WEIGHT TODAY: DAYS IN NICU:

CARES + HOLDING:

PROCEDURES:

NOTES + THOUGHTS:

Mighty Little One

TODAY I AM GRATEFUL FOR:

PRAYERS FOR PREEMIE:

Mighty Little One

DATE:

BABY'S WEIGHT TODAY: DAYS IN NICU:

CARES + HOLDING:

PROCEDURES:

NOTES + THOUGHTS:

Mighty Little One

TODAY I AM GRATEFUL FOR:

PRAYERS FOR PREEMIE:

Mighty Little One

DATE:

BABY'S WEIGHT TODAY: DAYS IN NICU:

CARES + HOLDING:

PROCEDURES:

NOTES + THOUGHTS:

Mighty Little One

TODAY I AM GRATEFUL FOR:

PRAYERS FOR PREEMIE:

Do not despise small Beginnings

ZECHARIA 4:10

Little but Fierce

Mighty Little One

DATE:

BABY'S WEIGHT TODAY: DAYS IN NICU:

CARES + HOLDING:

PROCEDURES:

NOTES + THOUGHTS:

Mighty Little One

TODAY I AM GRATEFUL FOR:

PRAYERS FOR PREEMIE:

Mighty Little One

DATE:

BABY'S WEIGHT TODAY: DAYS IN NICU:

CARES + HOLDING:

PROCEDURES:

NOTES + THOUGHTS:

Mighty Little One

TODAY I AM GRATEFUL FOR:

PRAYERS FOR PREEMIE:

Mighty Little One

DATE:

BABY'S WEIGHT TODAY: DAYS IN NICU:

CARES + HOLDING:

PROCEDURES:

NOTES + THOUGHTS:

Mighty Little One

TODAY I AM GRATEFUL FOR:

PRAYERS FOR PREEMIE:

Mighty Little One

DATE:

BABY'S WEIGHT TODAY: DAYS IN NICU:

CARES + HOLDING:

PROCEDURES:

NOTES + THOUGHTS:

Mighty Little One

TODAY I AM GRATEFUL FOR:

PRAYERS FOR PREEMIE:

Mighty Little One

DATE:

BABY'S WEIGHT TODAY: DAYS IN NICU:

CARES + HOLDING:

PROCEDURES:

NOTES + THOUGHTS:

Mighty Little One

TODAY I AM GRATEFUL FOR:

PRAYERS FOR PREEMIE:

I can do all things through Christ who gives me Strength

PHILIPPIANS 4:13

Preemie Strong

Mighty Little One

DATE:

BABY'S WEIGHT TODAY: DAYS IN NICU:

CARES + HOLDING:

PROCEDURES:

NOTES + THOUGHTS:

Mighty Little One

TODAY I AM GRATEFUL FOR:

PRAYERS FOR PREEMIE:

Mighty Little One

DATE:

BABY'S WEIGHT TODAY: DAYS IN NICU:

CARES + HOLDING:

PROCEDURES:

NOTES + THOUGHTS:

Mighty Little One

TODAY I AM GRATEFUL FOR:

PRAYERS FOR PREEMIE:

Mighty Little One

DATE:

BABY'S WEIGHT TODAY: DAYS IN NICU:

CARES + HOLDING:

PROCEDURES:

NOTES + THOUGHTS:

Mighty Little One

TODAY I AM GRATEFUL FOR:

PRAYERS FOR PREEMIE:

Mighty Little One

DATE:

BABY'S WEIGHT TODAY: DAYS IN NICU:

CARES + HOLDING:

PROCEDURES:

NOTES + THOUGHTS:

Mighty Little One

TODAY I AM GRATEFUL FOR:

PRAYERS FOR PREEMIE:

Mighty Little One

DATE:

BABY'S WEIGHT TODAY: DAYS IN NICU:

CARES + HOLDING:

PROCEDURES:

NOTES + THOUGHTS:

Mighty Little One

TODAY I AM GRATEFUL FOR:

PRAYERS FOR PREEMIE:

For He will command his angels concerning you to guard you in all your Ways

PSALM 91:11

Fighter

Mighty Little One

DATE:

BABY'S WEIGHT TODAY: DAYS IN NICU:

CARES + HOLDING:

PROCEDURES:

NOTES + THOUGHTS:

Mighty Little One

TODAY I AM GRATEFUL FOR:

PRAYERS FOR PREEMIE:

Mighty Little One

DATE:

BABY'S WEIGHT TODAY: DAYS IN NICU:

CARES + HOLDING:

PROCEDURES:

NOTES + THOUGHTS:

Mighty Little One

TODAY I AM GRATEFUL FOR:

PRAYERS FOR PREEMIE:

Mighty Little One

DATE:

BABY'S WEIGHT TODAY: DAYS IN NICU:

CARES + HOLDING:

PROCEDURES:

NOTES + THOUGHTS:

Mighty Little One

TODAY I AM GRATEFUL FOR:

PRAYERS FOR PREEMIE:

Mighty Little One

DATE:

BABY'S WEIGHT TODAY: DAYS IN NICU:

CARES + HOLDING:

PROCEDURES:

NOTES + THOUGHTS:

Mighty Little One

TODAY I AM GRATEFUL FOR:

PRAYERS FOR PREEMIE:

Mighty Little One

DATE:

BABY'S WEIGHT TODAY: DAYS IN NICU:

CARES + HOLDING:

PROCEDURES:

NOTES + THOUGHTS:

Mighty Little One

TODAY I AM GRATEFUL FOR:

PRAYERS FOR PREEMIE:

Whoever dwells in the shadow of the most high will abide in the shadow of the Almighty

PSALM 91:1

Tiny but Mighty

Mighty Little One

DATE:

BABY'S WEIGHT TODAY: DAYS IN NICU:

CARES + HOLDING:

PROCEDURES:

NOTES + THOUGHTS:

Mighty Little One

TODAY I AM GRATEFUL FOR:

PRAYERS FOR PREEMIE:

Mighty Little One

DATE:

BABY'S WEIGHT TODAY: DAYS IN NICU:

CARES + HOLDING:

PROCEDURES:

NOTES + THOUGHTS:

Mighty Little One

TODAY I AM GRATEFUL FOR:

PRAYERS FOR PREEMIE:

Mighty Little One

DATE:

BABY'S WEIGHT TODAY: DAYS IN NICU:

CARES + HOLDING:

PROCEDURES:

NOTES + THOUGHTS:

Mighty Little One

TODAY I AM GRATEFUL FOR:

PRAYERS FOR PREEMIE:

Mighty Little One

DATE:

BABY'S WEIGHT TODAY: DAYS IN NICU:

CARES + HOLDING:

PROCEDURES:

NOTES + THOUGHTS:

Mighty Little One

TODAY I AM GRATEFUL FOR:

PRAYERS FOR PREEMIE:

Mighty Little One

DATE:

BABY'S WEIGHT TODAY: DAYS IN NICU:

CARES + HOLDING:

PROCEDURES:

NOTES + THOUGHTS:

Mighty Little One

TODAY I AM GRATEFUL FOR:

PRAYERS FOR PREEMIE:

He shall cover you with His feathers and under His wings shall you trust, His truth shall be your shield and Buckler

PSALM 91:4

Baby

Brave

Mighty Little One

DATE:

BABY'S WEIGHT TODAY: DAYS IN NICU:

CARES + HOLDING:

PROCEDURES:

NOTES + THOUGHTS:

Mighty Little One

TODAY I AM GRATEFUL FOR:

PRAYERS FOR PREEMIE:

Mighty Little One

DATE:

BABY'S WEIGHT TODAY: DAYS IN NICU:

CARES + HOLDING:

PROCEDURES:

NOTES + THOUGHTS:

Mighty Little One

TODAY I AM GRATEFUL FOR:

PRAYERS FOR PREEMIE:

Mighty Little One

DATE:

BABY'S WEIGHT TODAY: DAYS IN NICU:

CARES + HOLDING:

PROCEDURES:

NOTES + THOUGHTS:

Mighty Little One

TODAY I AM GRATEFUL FOR:

PRAYERS FOR PREEMIE:

Mighty Little One

DATE:

BABY'S WEIGHT TODAY: DAYS IN NICU:

CARES + HOLDING:

PROCEDURES:

NOTES + THOUGHTS:

Mighty Little One

TODAY I AM GRATEFUL FOR:

PRAYERS FOR PREEMIE:

Mighty Little One

DATE:

BABY'S WEIGHT TODAY: DAYS IN NICU:

CARES + HOLDING:

PROCEDURES:

NOTES + THOUGHTS:

Mighty Little One

TODAY I AM GRATEFUL FOR:

PRAYERS FOR PREEMIE:

So do not fear,
for I am with you. Do not be
dismayed, for I am your God.
I will strengthen you and
help you. I will uphold you
with my righteous
right Hand.

ISAIAH 41:10

Courageous

Mighty Little One

DATE:

BABY'S WEIGHT TODAY: DAYS IN NICU:

CARES + HOLDING:

PROCEDURES:

NOTES + THOUGHTS:

Mighty Little One

TODAY I AM GRATEFUL FOR:

PRAYERS FOR PREEMIE:

Mighty Little One

DATE:

BABY'S WEIGHT TODAY: DAYS IN NICU:

CARES + HOLDING:

PROCEDURES:

NOTES + THOUGHTS:

Mighty Little One

TODAY I AM GRATEFUL FOR:

PRAYERS FOR PREEMIE:

Mighty Little One

DATE:

BABY'S WEIGHT TODAY: DAYS IN NICU:

CARES + HOLDING:

PROCEDURES:

NOTES + THOUGHTS:

Mighty Little One

TODAY I AM GRATEFUL FOR:

PRAYERS FOR PREEMIE:

Mighty Little One

DATE:

BABY'S WEIGHT TODAY: DAYS IN NICU:

CARES + HOLDING:

PROCEDURES:

NOTES + THOUGHTS:

Mighty Little One

TODAY I AM GRATEFUL FOR:

PRAYERS FOR PREEMIE:

Mighty Little One

DATE:

BABY'S WEIGHT TODAY: DAYS IN NICU:

CARES + HOLDING:

PROCEDURES:

NOTES + THOUGHTS:

Mighty Little One

TODAY I AM GRATEFUL FOR:

PRAYERS FOR PREEMIE:

But the Lord stood with me and strengthened Me

TIMOTHY 4:17

Nicu Warrior

Mighty Little One

DATE:

BABY'S WEIGHT TODAY: DAYS IN NICU:

CARES + HOLDING:

PROCEDURES:

NOTES + THOUGHTS:

Mighty Little One

TODAY I AM GRATEFUL FOR:

PRAYERS FOR PREEMIE:

Mighty Little One

DATE:

BABY'S WEIGHT TODAY: DAYS IN NICU:

CARES + HOLDING:

PROCEDURES:

NOTES + THOUGHTS:

Mighty Little One

TODAY I AM GRATEFUL FOR:

PRAYERS FOR PREEMIE:

Mighty Little One

DATE:

BABY'S WEIGHT TODAY: DAYS IN NICU:

CARES + HOLDING:

PROCEDURES:

NOTES + THOUGHTS:

Mighty Little One

TODAY I AM GRATEFUL FOR:

PRAYERS FOR PREEMIE:

Mighty Little One

DATE:

BABY'S WEIGHT TODAY: DAYS IN NICU:

CARES + HOLDING:

PROCEDURES:

NOTES + THOUGHTS:

Mighty Little One

TODAY I AM GRATEFUL FOR:

PRAYERS FOR PREEMIE:

Mighty Little One

DATE:

BABY'S WEIGHT TODAY: DAYS IN NICU:

CARES + HOLDING:

PROCEDURES:

NOTES + THOUGHTS:

Mighty Little One

TODAY I AM GRATEFUL FOR:

PRAYERS FOR PREEMIE:

Be still and know that I am with You

PSALM 46:10

Fight

Size

Mighty Little One

DATE:

BABY'S WEIGHT TODAY: DAYS IN NICU:

CARES + HOLDING:

PROCEDURES:

NOTES + THOUGHTS:

Mighty Little One

TODAY I AM GRATEFUL FOR:

PRAYERS FOR PREEMIE:

Mighty Little One

DATE:

BABY'S WEIGHT TODAY: DAYS IN NICU:

CARES + HOLDING:

PROCEDURES:

NOTES + THOUGHTS:

Mighty Little One

TODAY I AM GRATEFUL FOR:

PRAYERS FOR PREEMIE:

Mighty Little One

DATE:

BABY'S WEIGHT TODAY: DAYS IN NICU:

CARES + HOLDING:

PROCEDURES:

NOTES + THOUGHTS:

Mighty Little One

TODAY I AM GRATEFUL FOR:

PRAYERS FOR PREEMIE:

Mighty Little One

DATE:

BABY'S WEIGHT TODAY: DAYS IN NICU:

CARES + HOLDING:

PROCEDURES:

NOTES + THOUGHTS:

Mighty Little One

TODAY I AM GRATEFUL FOR:

PRAYERS FOR PREEMIE:

Mighty Little One

DATE:

BABY'S WEIGHT TODAY: DAYS IN NICU:

CARES + HOLDING:

PROCEDURES:

NOTES + THOUGHTS:

Mighty Little One

TODAY I AM GRATEFUL FOR:

PRAYERS FOR PREEMIE:

Be strong and Courageous

JOSHUA 1:9

Survivor

Mighty Little One

DATE:

BABY'S WEIGHT TODAY: DAYS IN NICU:

CARES + HOLDING:

PROCEDURES:

NOTES + THOUGHTS:

Mighty Little One

TODAY I AM GRATEFUL FOR:

PRAYERS FOR PREEMIE:

Mighty Little One

DATE:

BABY'S WEIGHT TODAY: DAYS IN NICU:

CARES + HOLDING:

PROCEDURES:

NOTES + THOUGHTS:

Mighty Little One

TODAY I AM GRATEFUL FOR:

PRAYERS FOR PREEMIE:

Mighty Little One

DATE:

BABY'S WEIGHT TODAY: DAYS IN NICU:

CARES + HOLDING:

PROCEDURES:

NOTES + THOUGHTS:

Mighty Little One

TODAY I AM GRATEFUL FOR:

PRAYERS FOR PREEMIE:

Mighty Little One

DATE:

BABY'S WEIGHT TODAY: DAYS IN NICU:

CARES + HOLDING:

PROCEDURES:

NOTES + THOUGHTS:

Mighty Little One

TODAY I AM GRATEFUL FOR:

PRAYERS FOR PREEMIE:

Mighty Little One

DATE:

BABY'S WEIGHT TODAY: DAYS IN NICU:

CARES + HOLDING:

PROCEDURES:

NOTES + THOUGHTS:

Mighty Little One

TODAY I AM GRATEFUL FOR:

PRAYERS FOR PREEMIE:

The Lord bless
you and keep
You

NUMBERS 6:22

Mighty

Miracle

Mighty Little One

DATE:

BABY'S WEIGHT TODAY: DAYS IN NICU:

CARES + HOLDING:

PROCEDURES:

NOTES + THOUGHTS:

Mighty Little One

TODAY I AM GRATEFUL FOR:

PRAYERS FOR PREEMIE:

Mighty Little One

DATE:

BABY'S WEIGHT TODAY: DAYS IN NICU:

CARES + HOLDING:

PROCEDURES:

NOTES + THOUGHTS:

Mighty Little One

TODAY I AM GRATEFUL FOR:

PRAYERS FOR PREEMIE:

Mighty Little One

DATE:

BABY'S WEIGHT TODAY: DAYS IN NICU:

CARES + HOLDING:

PROCEDURES:

NOTES + THOUGHTS:

Mighty Little One

TODAY I AM GRATEFUL FOR:

PRAYERS FOR PREEMIE:

Mighty Little One

DATE:

BABY'S WEIGHT TODAY: DAYS IN NICU:

CARES + HOLDING:

PROCEDURES:

NOTES + THOUGHTS:

Mighty Little One

TODAY I AM GRATEFUL FOR:

PRAYERS FOR PREEMIE:

Mighty Little One

DATE:

BABY'S WEIGHT TODAY: DAYS IN NICU:

CARES + HOLDING:

PROCEDURES:

NOTES + THOUGHTS:

Mighty Little One

TODAY I AM GRATEFUL FOR:

PRAYERS FOR PREEMIE:

Nicu Milestones

First milk feed   Date:

First cuddle with mom   Date:

First cuddle with dad   Date:

Had my first bath   Date:

Doubled my birth weight   Date:

First time wearing clothes   Date:

Moved to my own crib   Date:

One month old   Date:

Completely off CPAP   Date:

Breathing on my own   Date:

Reached my due date   Date:

First time at the breast   Date:

Going H♡ME!!   Date:

For you formed my inward parts

You knitted me together in my mother's womb.

I praise you for I am fearfully and wonderfully made

PSALM 139:13-14:

Mighty Little One

Mighty Little One

Mighty Little One

Get to know the author's journey through baby
loss, rainbows and miracles

Made in the USA
Coppell, TX
03 April 2022

75855428R00086